AF691576

THE GOSPEL OF GOLD

THE GOSPEL OF GOLD

KAYLEE YORK

Kaylee York
The Gospel of Gold

All rights reserved
Copyright © 2026 by Kaylee York

No part of this publication may be reproduced, distributed, or transmitted in any form or by any means, including photocopying, recording, or other electronic or mechanical methods, without the prior written permission of the publisher, except in the case of brief quotations embodied in critical reviews and certain other noncommercial uses permitted by copyright law.

Published by Spines
ISBN: 979-8-90418-515-2

Spines

CHAPTER I: THE SUN-METAL AND THE HUNGER OF MEN

Gold, this sun-fragment fallen into the hands of mortals, has ruled more tyrants than any crown forged upon an anvil. It gleams with an insolence that mocks the fragility of the creatures who desire it. How small a human hand is, and yet how it trembles when it closes around this cold eternity! Gold does not shine; it accuses. For what is gold if not the mirror in which mankind first saw its own hunger made divine? Not the hunger of the stomach, but the deeper, secret famine, the yearning for permanence, for dominion, for the feeling of being more than a fleeting breath in the endless exhalation of the cosmos.

It is a metal that reflects the will to power far more faithfully than any scripture ever dared. Gold says nothing, yet it commands more fervently than prophets. Gold promises nothing, yet men beg before it. Gold needs nothing, and that is why men need it. Observe the paradox: gold nourishes no body, shelters no child, rescues no wounded, yet civilizations have bled themselves dry to possess it. Why? Because gold is the one thing that refuses to decay. In its stubborn radiance, men see the insult of their own impermanence. They crumble; gold endures. And in this endurance they detect a hidden promise: "Take me, and you too may endure."

But what small spirits imagine endurance to be! They mistake preservation for greatness, and hoarding for triumph. The weak cling to gold as a drowning man clings to driftwood, not because it will save him, but because he cannot imagine the sea bearing him up by his own strength. Gold is not the corrupter of men; it is the revealer of men.

For the one who seeks gold as a master finds himself its slave. For the one who wields it as a tool finds his own will sharpened. Consider the conqueror: he surrounds himself with gold not to worship it, but to remind the world of his victories. His gold is the echo of his footsteps across the earth. But the merchant who worships his own coffers is merely a prisoner of the coins he kisses; he is buried alive beneath the weight of his own longing. The world mistakes them for kin, but they are as different as the sun and the candle that imitates it.

And thus the first truth of the sun-metal emerges: Gold does not elevate the man, it magnifies him. Whatever he carries within, ambition or fear, creativity or cowardice, gold amplifies. He who is great with little gold becomes greater with much. He who is small with little gold becomes smaller still. Therefore, let the seeker of gold be warned: gold is not an escape from the self, but a confrontation with it. Many imagine they seek wealth, but in truth they flee from the emptiness within their own breast. They hope that the reflected light of gold will fill it, but gold reflects everything except the void.

And so begins this philosophy of gold, not a chronicle of its mining nor a ledger of its price, but an inquiry into its ancient spell. Gold, the metal that does not rust, that does not surrender, that does not bend: an incorruptible judge placed in the hands of a corruptible species.

What does gold awaken?

What does it demand?

What does it reveal about those who dare to possess it?

For every age returns to this same lesson, stumbling as if for the first time: Gold is not a treasure. It is a test.

CHAPTER II: OF STELLAR ASH AND THE LONG DESCENT OF FIRE

Before gold ever learned the weight of a human palm, it endured immensities that would shatter every throne and temple ever raised in its name. Let us strip gold of its coinage and its crowns for a moment and return it to its true ancestry. For gold is not born of earth. Earth is merely its last refuge.

In the beginning, if such a phrase may be forgiven, there was no gold. There were only young stars, ravenous furnaces devouring hydrogen, forging light from pressure, and time from flame. These stars were creators, yes, but modest ones. They could make iron, but no further. And iron, that proud metal of swords and rails, marked a limit, a wall beyond which ordinary creation could not pass. To forge gold requires not growth, but catastrophe.

Gold is the child of stellar violence.

When a massive star exhausts its fuel and collapses under its own ambition, when gravity finally overcomes fusion's fragile truce, the universe commits an act of terrible generosity. A supernova tears the star apart, hurling its inner secrets into the void. In that instant. Brief, furious, unrepeatable. Conditions arise so extreme that nature forgets its restraint. Atomic nuclei are bombarded, overloaded, forced into heavier and rarer forms. Here, in this cosmic convulsion, gold is born. Not gently, but as shrapnel. Not as craft, but as excess.

Thus gold begins its existence not as a symbol of order, but as evidence of chaos overcome.

Cast outward at unimaginable speed, these newborn atoms wander for billions of years. They drift through cold darkness, indifferent to planets, unaware of life, untouched by valuation. They are patient beyond morality. They wait while galaxies spin like thoughts half-formed. They wait while dust thickens, while gravity gathers, while worlds slowly coagulate from debris and chance.

Eventually, after epochs that mock all human calendars, some of this ancient ash falls into the forming Earth. The planet is young, molten, restless. Gold, heavy and obedient to gravity, sinks toward the core like a truth too dense for the surface. Most of it remains there still, locked away beyond reach, laughing silently at all our mining and measuring. What men possess is only the scrapings, the accidents, the crumbs shaken loose by violence.

For gold reaches the surface only through further upheaval. Through tectonic cruelty. Through pressure, heat, and fracture. Through water that dissolves and redeposits, again and again, with a patience that rivals the stars themselves. Gold rises not because it is chosen, but because the Earth is wounded. Veins form where rock breaks. Nuggets settle where rivers tire. Gold appears where the planet has suffered long enough.

And now, at last, the metal meets man.

What a meeting of misunderstandings! Man imagines

he has discovered gold. Gold knows it has merely arrived late.

Consider the arrogance of the miner, who believes he extracts value from stone. He does not know that he interrupts a journey already billions of years in motion. His pick is a punctuation mark in a sentence written before life learned to speak. The gold in his hand has outlived entire species. It has crossed interstellar emptiness. It has survived annihilation. And now it tolerates being weighed in ounces.

This is the true irony: men worship gold for its permanence, yet fail to comprehend the scale of that permanence. They treat it as treasure when it is testimony. Gold does not testify to human greatness, but to human smallness. It whispers: *I was ancient before your ancestors learned fear. I will remain when your names have evaporated.*

And yet, here lies the deeper cruelty. Man is not wrong to feel awe. For gold is one of the few things he touches that was not made for him, not shaped by his need, not responsive to his prayers. It resists him not by force, but by indifference. Gold does not care whether it is crown or circuit, idol or ingot. It submits equally to tyrant and artist. It waits.

Thus gold on the ground beneath our feet is not merely metal. It is condensed time. It is stellar memory made dense enough to bruise the world. It is the echo of explosions older than the Earth, resting quietly in riverbeds and mountains, pretending to be inert.

And when men fight over it, spill blood for it, lie for it, kneel before it, they enact a strange reversal. The ephemeral wars over the eternal fragment. The mayflies disputing ownership of a fallen star.

Here, then, is the second truth of the sun-metal:

Gold is not rare because the Earth is stingy.

Gold is rare because the universe is extravagant only in moments of destruction.

To desire gold is to desire a piece of catastrophe made calm. To hold it is to hold proof that creation itself required ruin. And perhaps this is why gold unsettles us so deeply. It reminds us that greatness is born not from comfort, but from collapse.

Gold did not fall to Earth to save mankind. It fell because a star died.

And mankind, finding it at last, mistook an epitaph for a promise.

CHAPTER III: OF GODS, GRAVES, AND GILDED LIES

Gold did not enter history quietly. It announced itself wherever humans first dared to imagine eternity. Long before empires learned to count, before alphabets learned to remember, gold was already whispering to the dead.

The earliest hands to shape it belonged not to kings, but to priests and mourners. In the graves of the ancient Balkans, Varna, that forgotten threshold of civilization, gold lay beside skeletons whose names dissolved five thousand years ago. These were not ornaments of vanity. They were bribes for the afterlife. The first civilization we know to work gold did not ask, *What can this buy?* They asked, *What can this carry beyond death?*

Here gold became what it has always secretly wished to be: a passport to permanence.

To bury gold with the dead was to declare a rebellion against decay. Flesh rots, bone powders, memory thins, but gold endures. In placing it among corpses, early man enacted a metaphysical gamble: that what does not perish might escort what must. Gold was not wealth; it was hope hammered into form. The dead were armed not with weapons, but with incorruptibility.

From there, gold ascended naturally into divinity. The Egyptians, those supreme aesthetes of eternity, understood this best. Their gods were golden not because gold was beautiful, but because it was *unchanging*. Gold was the flesh of the sun, and the sun was the daily proof that death could be defeated. At least not symbolically. Pharaohs did not wear gold to display power; they wore it to deny mortality. Their tombs were not storage rooms, but arguments against time itself.

Thus gold became theology made visible.

Yet wherever gold becomes sacred, hierarchy soon follows. The temples glittered while the people bowed. The metal that promised transcendence also perfected domination. Priests claimed communion with gods because they alone handled the divine substance. Gold separated the initiated from the herd, the eternal from the expendable. Already the pattern was set: gold would always speak in two tongues. Salvation for the few, submission for the many.

Centuries passed. Gods multiplied, then weakened. But gold adapted. When faith migrated from temples to texts, gold followed obediently. In the medieval world, where parchment replaced stone and scripture replaced myth, gold learned a new vocation: illumination.

Monks bent over manuscripts, tracing divine words with powdered sun. Gold leaf crowned letters not for readability, but for reverence. The message was unmistakable: *This text does not belong to the world of dirt and hunger.* Gold transformed words into relics. Truth, they implied, must shine. Holiness must reflect light. And so gold disciplined belief, teaching the eye what the soul was meant to obey.

But even here, the metal betrayed its neutrality. While peasants prayed before golden pages they would never touch, kings and bishops counted coin. Gold bridged heaven and treasury with disturbing ease. It sanctified authority while financing war. No contradiction troubled it. Gold has never suffered from conscience.

Then came the modern sickness: ideology.

In the twentieth century, when gods were declared dead and nations demanded myths in their place, gold was conscripted once more. The Nazis, those desperate architects of invented antiquity, reached backward into mist and rune. Gold was summoned as evidence. Ancient artifacts, imagined lineages, fabricated continuity. Hitler's propagandists paraded gold as proof of a primordial Aryan destiny, tying Celts, Teutons, and mythic ancestors into a single glowing lie.

Here gold did not sanctify gods, but race.

It shimmered in museums and ceremonies as validation: *We were always meant to rule.* That the metal itself came from exploded stars mattered little. What mattered was that it looked ancient, immutable, authoritative. Gold became propaganda fossilized into shine. A lie made heavier by brilliance.

And then something unexpected happened. Gold abandoned myth.

Not entirely, never entirely, but it learned to speak a new language: function. In the 1970s, quietly, without ceremony, gold entered the circuitry of machines. No priests. No kings. No banners. Just engineers. Gold proved useful not because it was eternal, but because it was obedient. It conducted without corroding. It connected without betraying. Inside microchips, gold became invisible sovereignty. The unseen enabler of speed, memory, and calculation.

How fitting.

The metal once buried with corpses now pulsed through computers. The substance of tombs became the nervous system of modernity. Gold no longer crowned rulers; it synchronized clocks, stabilized signals, carried information at the speed of light. The sun-metal learned humility. Not moral humility, but technical necessity.

And today, gold sits everywhere and nowhere. In smartphones, satellites, medical implants, spacecraft drifting beyond Mars. It no longer announces itself. It hides. The age of spectacle has given way to the age of integration. Gold has become infrastructure.

Yet do not be deceived. The metaphysics remain.

We still trust gold because it does not change. We still embed it where failure is unacceptable. We still associate it with certainty in a world of volatility. The altar has shrunk to a circuit board, but the faith endures. Gold is still called upon where human error must be minimized, where decay is intolerable.

Thus the transformation is not a rejection, but a refinement. Gold has passed from god, to symbol, to lie, to tool.

And perhaps this is its most honest form.

For in machines, gold finally serves without pretending to redeem. It no longer promises salvation, race, or eternity. It simply works. And in that quiet usefulness, it exposes a truth more unsettling than any myth:

When stripped of illusion, gold is not meaning. It is reliability.

And mankind, having exhausted gods and ideologies alike, now worships what functions. Whether this marks our maturity or merely a new superstition remains unanswered.

But gold, ancient as catastrophe itself, will endure the verdict. It always does.

CHAPTER IV: OF ADORNMENT, DOMINION, AND THE FIRST LIE OF EXCHANGE

Power learned early that it must be seen before it can be obeyed. Long before law was written, before borders were drawn, before crowns were named, there was already ornament. Gold was the first grammar of authority.

The earliest kingdoms did not mint coins; they adorned bodies. In Mesopotamia, in Egypt, in the Indus and along the Danube, gold announced distinction before hierarchy could explain itself.

The chieftain wore it so the crowd would not confuse him with themselves. The priest wore it so the gods would recognize their interpreter. Gold became the visible argument for invisible superiority.

Status required distance, and gold created distance effortlessly.

Why jewelry? Because the body is the first altar. To place gold upon flesh was to declare that this flesh was not like others. Neck, wrist, brow. These were not decorative choices but symbolic territories. The neck bore submission or command. The wrist controlled labor. The brow housed judgment. To gild these places was to announce sovereignty over work, violence, and decision itself.

Gold jewelry was not fashion; it was theology worn as fact.

And it spread for a simple reason: gold does not lie about endurance. Wood rots. Bone cracks. Bronze dulls. Gold remains. To wear it was to steal a fragment of eternity and fasten it to the self. Kings understood this instinctively. Their enemies might kill them, but portraits would survive. Tombs would shine. Memory, that fragile tyrant, would be bribed with metal.

Yet adornment alone was not enough. As societies grew complex, gold learned a colder role. It ceased to merely *signal* power and began to *measure* it.

Thus currency was born. Not from trade, but from control.

The first gold currencies did not emerge in bustling markets among equals. They emerged under rulers who demanded taxes, soldiers who demanded pay, and states that demanded obedience. Lydia, that pragmatic genius of domination, stamped gold into coins not to empower merchants, but to standardize submission. A stamped coin said: *This weight is sanctioned. This value is decreed. This symbol speaks for authority.*

Currency was jewelry stripped of intimacy and armed with law.

Ancient rules were strict because trust was fragile. Weight was sacred. Purity was inspected. Debasement was heresy. To tamper with gold currency was not merely fraud; it was sacrilege against the state. Markets did not yet float; they were anchored. Exchange occurred face to face, metal to metal, trust to trust. Gold did not represent value, it *was* value. No abstraction intervened.

And so gold disciplined desire. You could not conjure it from promises. You could not multiply it with words. You either had it or you did not. Power accumulated slowly, visibly, brutally.

Inequality was honest.

Compare this to the modern carnival.

Today, gold no longer circulates hand to hand like a verdict passed between palms. It sits behind glass, behind digits, behind derivatives. Its weight has been translated into contracts, ETFs, futures, spot prices blinking across screens like nervous thoughts. Gold is exchanged without being touched, owned without being seen, pledged without being moved.

The ancient man weighed gold to test truth. The modern man prices gold to test belief.

Once, gold ruled by presence. Now it rules by reference.

Collateralized, leveraged, and rehypothecated, gold has been stretched thin across financial architectures its original makers would have judged as sorcery or madness. It is loaned without leaving vaults, sold without changing hands, promised to many while resting in one place. The ancient rules of purity and possession have dissolved into probabilistic ownership.

Where once gold restrained power, it now lubricates it.

Loans backed by gold no longer demand the metal's movement, only its shadow. Markets trade "spot" as though immediacy still exists, though settlement drifts and obligations stack like unconfessed sins. Gold has become a language spoken fluently by machines, arbitraged by algorithms, and rarely questioned by those who trust the abstraction more than the substance.

And yet, notice this carefully. The instinct has not changed.

Jewelry still signals status. Gold chains still shout where words are insufficient. Nations still boast reserves as ancient kings once boasted crowns. In moments of panic, men still flee paper and return to metal, as if running back to an old god whose silence feels safer than new promises.

The rules have changed, but the hunger has not.

Gold was once worn to be seen. Then it was stamped to be trusted. Now it is priced to be believed.

Each stage reveals not gold's evolution, but man's.

For gold has remained stubbornly itself. Dense, mute, incorruptible. It is mankind who has grown abstract, remote, and anxious. We no longer dare to touch what we claim to own. We accept representations where once we demanded weight.

And so the final irony emerges:

The more sophisticated our markets become, the more primitive our faith reveals itself to be.

For beneath every contract, every collateralized loan, every flashing spot price, there still lies the same ancient confession:

We trust gold because we do not trust ourselves.

Gold, once jewelry for kings, then law for states, now floats as a ghost through financial systems. Still sovereign, still desired, still accusing.

It has not lost its power.

It has merely learned to rule without being seen.

CHAPTER V: OF LATTICES, SILENCE, AND THE GEOMETRY OF FREEDOM

Only now may we speak of structure.

Not earlier. Not at the beginning. For to begin with structure would have been an obscenity, like explaining the skeleton to one who has not yet learned reverence for the living body. Gold does not reveal its inner order to the impatient. Respect must be earned before meaning appears.

Gold has an architecture.

Beneath its smooth defiance, beneath the surface that refuses rust and apology, gold arranges itself in perfect obedience to number. Its atoms fall into a face-centered cubic lattice, each point precisely spaced, each relation exact, each angle without improvisation. Nothing here is symbolic. Nothing negotiates. Gold is not chaotic matter pretending to be orderly; it is order incarnate.

This is why gold conducts without hesitation, reflects without distortion, endures without fatigue. Its crystalline structure is not merely physical, it is moral. Gold does not improvise. It does not decay into alternatives. It does not argue with mathematics. It *accepts* necessity.

And herein lies the first metaphysical provocation:

Gold behaves as though it remembers the laws that made it.

The same impossible precision that governed its birth in stellar catastrophe governs its atomic stillness now. The universe did not relax after the explosion; it merely condensed its discipline. What once occurred in violent excess now persists as silent symmetry. Gold is catastrophe reconciled into geometry.

Cosmic Formation Sequence Gold does not primarily arise from ordinary stellar fusion. It emerges when matter is forced beyond equilibrium in extreme astrophysical events. The journey of gold can be summarized through a chain of matter-states and transformations. Matter-states (S):

S0 = Light elements (H, He)

S1 = Iron-peak seed nuclei

S2 = Neutron-rich heavy isotopes

S3 = Stable gold (197Au)

S4 = Interstellar dust / proto-solar nebula

S5 = Terrestrial ores and placers

S6 = Crystalline gold (FCC)

Transformation chain:

S0 -> S1 -> S2 -> S3 -> S4 -> S5 -> S6

Nuclear core processes:

Neutron capture: (Z, A) + n -> (Z, A+1) Beta decay: (Z, A) -> (Z+1, A) + electron + antineutrino.

Is it any wonder, then, that human consciousness senses something familiar here?

For consciousness itself, whatever else it may be, is also structure emerging from violence. Neurons fire because of gradients, thresholds, probabilities. Thought arises not from chaos, but from patterned constraint. Awareness is not freedom from law; it is law complex enough to reflect upon itself.

Thus gold unsettles us. Its crystalline order mirrors an aspiration buried deep within the mind: the longing to be structured without being enslaved, governed without being diminished.

Gold achieves what man only dreams of. It is bound by law, yet sovereign.

Here the metaphysical temptation begins.

If consciousness is not random, but patterned; if awareness emerges from mathematical precision layered upon time; then gold becomes more than metal. It becomes a reminder that meaning does not oppose structure, it *requires* it. The mystics sensed this without equations. The alchemists fumbled toward it with symbols. They intuited that gold was not merely matter perfected, but *matter remembering itself.*

The philosopher's stone was never about transmutation of lead. It was about alignment—bringing the chaotic self into resonance with the hidden order of the world.

Gold, in its crystalline calm, already lives there. Now we may speak of freedom.

Not the childish freedom of indulgence, nor the theatrical freedom of slogans, but the rare and dangerous freedom that depends on conditions. Gold does not promise freedom universally. It offers freedom *situationally.* Those who own gold own optionality—the ability to move, to wait, to refuse, to survive unfavorable climates of power.

Gold does not liberate the world. It liberates *position.*

In times of stability, gold appears inert, even foolish.

Paper multiplies faster. Credit smiles wider. But when climates shift from political, to monetary, to civil, gold reasserts its older authority. Its value is not intrinsic in isolation; it is relational, tethered to uncertainty. Gold is freedom calibrated to disorder.

Thus those who hold gold do not escape history. They hedge against its mood swings.

This is why tyrants hoard it and dissidents bury it. Why empires stockpile it and refugees sew it into clothing. Gold does not take sides. It equips whoever anticipates rupture. It is the metal of contingency.

And here we must confess why this chapter arrives late.

To speak of gold's crystalline metaphysics before its violence, its burial with the dead, its corruption by power, its humiliation into circuitry. This would have produced mysticism without gravity. Reverence without weight. One must first understand that gold was born in explosion, worshipped in fear, abused in lies, disciplined into function. Only then may one appreciate its inner stillness.

Gold's structure is not innocence. It is *earned silence.*

Those who rush to spiritualize gold without honoring its origin mistake reflection for revelation. They want transcendence without catastrophe, meaning without cost. But gold teaches otherwise. Order emerges only after excess. Clarity only after annihilation. Freedom only after constraint.

This is the final, dangerous lesson of the sun-metal:

True freedom is not the absence of structure.

It is structure aligned so perfectly that resistance disappears.

Gold achieves this at the atomic level. Man glimpses it

only in rare moments of coherence when thought, action, and consequence briefly align.

Until then, gold waits.

Patient in its lattice. Indifferent to belief.

Silent with knowledge earned before language.

And it will outlast every metaphysical system erected prematurely around it.

As it always has.

CHAPTER VI: OF MAPS THAT DREAM AND THE PROPHECY BENEATH OUR FEET

There is a superstition that the Earth has already given up her secrets. This belief comforts the lazy and flatters the powerful. But the ground has not been exhausted. Only patience has.

Gold does not scatter itself at random. It remembers where it has been wounded.

Every vein, every placer, every hidden lode is a scar left by violence older than nations. Mountains rose, oceans fled, plates collided like drunken gods, and in the fractures gold paused. The Earth does not *hide* gold; it places it where stress once ruled. To know where gold will be found is not to guess, but to listen and to read the autobiography of stone.

Now mankind has learned to read differently.

Geological formations speak first. Cratons, the ancient, stable hearts of continents, guard the deepest secrets. Where the crust is old and thick, where time itself seems reluctant to move, gold accumulates patiently. Around these ancient cores, greenstone belts twist like fossilized lightning, recording primordial violence. Wherever continents once tore and healed, wherever magma rose and cooled under pressure, gold followed heat, fluids, and fracture with obedient inevitability.

Then comes dispersion. Rivers are not merely water; they are historians. They drag the past into the present grain by grain. Where rivers slow, gold waits. Where coastlines curve and currents tire, gold settles. The shape of land dictates the patience of water, and the patience of water dictates the resting places of metal.

Modern eyes now see what ancient feet merely stumbled upon.

Predictive GIS technology overlays this story with cold precision. Satellite data traces fault lines invisible to the naked eye. Magnetics reveal buried structures. Geochemical anomalies whisper of metals dissolved and redeposited long ago. Algorithms learn the patterns of known deposits and project them outward like shadows cast into the unknown. The Earth is no longer merely observed, it is interrogated.

And yet here lies the arrogance. Machines alone do not suffice. For before satellites, there were stories.

Indigenous populations, dismissed too long as myth-bearers rather than data-keepers, encoded geological memory in ritual and tale. Sacred mountains forbidden to disturb. Rivers said to "bleed yellow." Valleys where the sun was said to sleep beneath the soil. These were not metaphors born of ignorance. They were warnings born of familiarity. The land spoke to those who lived within its rhythms, and gold entered language long before it entered vaults.

Modern prediction emerges where these worlds overlap: stone, code, and story aligned.

When ancient oral maps coincide with tectonic stress zones; when ritual sites cluster near mineralized belts; when myths of "fire beneath the ground" echo volcanic arcs—gold listens. It is found not by conquest alone, but by coherence of understanding.

Thus new frontiers emerge. Not in oceans or stars, but beneath borders already drawn. And now the implications grow dangerous.

To predict gold is to predict power.

A nation that knows where gold lies knows where influence will someday flow. Infrastructure follows foresight. Roads, "development projects," conservation zones, and military bases appear not by coincidence, but by anticipation. What is framed as protection is often preparation. What is framed as peace is often positioning.

In war-time, predicted gold zones become strategic silence. Regions are destabilized, alliances strained, sovereignty questioned. Not because gold has been mined, but because it *could be*.

Control of future resources shapes present aggression more effectively than armies alone.

In economics, capital migrates before discovery. Land prices shift. Currencies hedge quietly. Corporations negotiate decades ahead of extraction. The market learns to trade on *potential*, and potential becomes leverage. Gold not yet unearthed already distorts balance sheets and treaties.

Territory, once defined by borders, is now defined by probability.

This is the new cartography: maps not of what is, but of what *will matter*.

And so gold resumes its ancient role, not merely as metal, but as oracle. Those who read the Earth correctly do not need to rush. They wait while others fight over surface illusions. They let history move toward the places where gravity, geology, and human desire will inevitably converge.

Yet beware the final irony.

The more accurately we predict gold, the less free we become. Surveillance replaces serendipity. Discovery becomes entitlement. The myth of chance dies, and with it a certain humility. We begin to believe the Earth owes us her riches because our models say so.

But gold has always punished entitlement.

The land may reveal where gold *can* be found—but not when it will tolerate being taken.

Thus the true wisdom is not prediction, but restraint. To know where gold sleeps is power. To decide when to wake it is responsibility. History shows that mankind excels at the first and fails catastrophically at the second.

The ground remembers every betrayal.

And gold, ancient witness to all empires, waits patiently in its fractures—unmoved by maps, unimpressed by machines, indifferent to flags until the next great conflict teaches mankind, once again, that foresight without wisdom is merely another form of blindness.

CHAPTER VII: OF THE PLACES WHERE GOLD STILL DREAMS

Gold is not discovered by desire. It is revealed by pressure. Geological, political, and moral. Those who understand *where* gold sleeps shape the future long before a single ounce is mined. And those who mistake possession for wisdom inevitably awaken it too early. Now we shall delve into the unmined or undermined potentials that our sacred crust cradles.

Begin in the cold silence of the **Eastern Siberian Craton**, where the Earth has forgotten to move. Here lies stone older than memory, a continental heart that has survived every fashion of extinction. Its structure mirrors the great gold-bearing cratons of history, yet it remains largely untouched. Not because it is barren, but because it is inhospitable. The gold here sleeps deeply, compressed by time and frost, guarded not by scarcity but by endurance. What is absent is not metal, but appetite willing to endure the cold politics and colder winters required to awaken it.

Travel then to the dense green concealment of the **Western Amazon Craton**, where gold announces itself only indirectly. Rivers carry whispers of it downstream, fine grains glittering in mud like forgotten syllables of a much older sentence. Indigenous stories speak of forbidden places, of yellow earth that demands respect. Modern instruments confirm what myth preserved: beneath jungle and sediment lies ancient shield geology, buried not by accident, but by time's deliberate attempt to hide its excesses.

Across the Atlantic, the **West African Birimian Belt** stretches like a half-read manuscript. Here gold has already revealed itself generously, yet only at the surface, like a tease. The deeper chapters remain closed. These rocks formed during violent accretionary epochs when the Earth was young and careless with abundance. What has been mined so far are merely the margins; the true weight remains locked below, awaiting either patience or desperation—two forces history supplies in abundance.

At the far edge of the world's long spine lies the **Patagonia Massif**, a land that looks empty only because man has not yet learned to see depth as presence. Beneath its windswept austerity, ancient magmatic systems intersect fault zones that have barely been tested. Gold here is not absent; it is aloof. It waits under stone that has not yet been sufficiently disturbed by ambition.

Northward again, beneath ice and silence, the **Northern Canadian Shield** continues its patient concealment. Glaciers scraped the surface clean, erasing obvious signs, but leaving intact what matters below. Geophysics sees what eyes cannot: greenstone belts extending beneath till, structures that elsewhere host vast gold systems. Here, the barrier is neither knowledge nor metal, but the human willingness to invest decades where returns refuse immediacy.

In the thin air of impossible altitude, the **Tibetan Plateau** bears scars of continental collision so extreme that the crust itself thickened in protest. Such pressure zones are alchemical kitchens, driving fluids through fractures deep enough to carry gold upward and trap it in silence. Much remains unexplored, not for lack of promise, but because power, altitude, and politics conspire to keep questions unasked.

At the heart of a continent already drunk on mineral success lies the **Central Australian Craton**. Here, the deception is familiarity. Because Australia is known for gold, its interior is assumed to be understood. It is not. Olympic Dam taught a brutal lesson: the richest truths lie beneath what appears exhausted. Gold in central Australia waits at depths that punish shallow thinking and reward only those who accept that discovery now belongs to endurance, not luck.

As ice retreats, it exposes not merely land but memory. The **Kalaallit Nunaat** shield—ancient, Archean, and long imprisoned beneath glaciers—is beginning to breathe again. What emerges is not new geology, but newly visible opportunity. Gold here has not been depleted; it has simply been hidden by climate. As ice yields, so too will the illusions that this land is empty.

Between empires, fractured by borders that never aligned with stone, stretches the **Central Asian Orogenic Belt**. It is one of the largest gold-bearing systems on Earth, yet remains strangely under-acknowledged. Here, tectonic chaos bred abundance, but political chaos obscured it. Gold persists regardless of flags, but access obeys them.

This region's future conflicts may not begin over ideology, but over what lies beneath it.

Finally, consider what lies unseen not because it is distant, but because it is submerged: the **Submerged Continental Shelves**. When sea levels rose, ancient river systems drowned, carrying their gold with them. These placers did not vanish; they merely slipped beneath a legal and technological horizon. Here lies gold untouched by history's violence, waiting for a species bold or foolish enough to claim it from the sea.

Thus the Earth still holds its reserves, not evenly, not kindly, but faithfully according to its own ancient logic. Gold gathers where turmoil once shaped stone, where time had patience, and where humanity hesitated. Those who learn to read these signs do not need prophecy. They already stand in the future, watching the present struggle toward them.

CHAPTER VIII: OF FORTRESSES, FIRE, AND THE METAL THAT TAUGHT MEN TO GUARD

Gold has never marched at the front of armies, yet armies have always marched for it. It does not shout commands, but it rearranges the feet of soldiers across continents. Wherever gold gathered, men learned a new instinct: to protect. And from that instinct arose walls, weapons, ranks, and the long education of violence we now call history.

In the earliest centuries, gold altered the very geometry of settlement. A village with no gold needed only neighbors. A village with gold needed sentries. What had once been a circle of huts became a perimeter; what had been communal became guarded. Gold did not create enemies —it *attracted* them. Thus the first protective forces were not born from conquest, but from fear of loss. Spears were sharpened not for glory, but for vigilance. Watchtowers rose not to see far, but to see *early*.

Where gold appeared, security followed like a shadow that learned to harden.

Territorial expansion soon discovered gold as its silent justification. Lands were not taken because they were empty, nor because they were beautiful, but because they were rumored to hold something that did not rot. A valley rich in grain fed a season; a valley rich in gold fed ambition. Armies learned the difference quickly. Campaigns bent toward rivers known to carry yellow dust, toward mountains whose stones whispered of veins. Borders became elastic wherever gold resisted ownership.

Gold taught men that territory was not merely space, but *potential.*

Processing followed power. To hold gold safely, one had to learn to tame it. Fire became not only warmth but instrument. Crushing stones, washing sediments, smelting concentrates—these were not crafts of leisure, but acts of discipline. Gold demanded precision. Too much heat ruined alloy. Too little left impurity. In learning to refine gold, men learned to refine themselves: patience, control, hierarchy. The forge became a school of command. Those who mastered fire ruled those who feared it.

Thus metallurgy and military order grew together, siblings raised by necessity.

Gold's softness taught another lesson. Unlike iron, it bent. Unlike bronze, it yielded. This made it useless for blades, but perfect for seals, insignia, standards. Gold marked authority rather than enforcing it. A general's weapon was iron; his authority was gold. One killed bodies, the other commanded loyalty. Soldiers followed banners not because they shone, but because they promised continuity—pay remembered, victories recorded, honor made tangible.

Gold stabilized allegiance long before coin standardized wages.

Fortresses arose where gold accumulated. Not because gold needed shelter from nature, but from man. Vaults were dug, walls thickened, access narrowed. Every layer of protection was an admission: *this metal is worth killing for*. In defending gold, societies rehearsed defense itself. The art of fortification matured around treasuries. The science of siege matured in response.

Gold refined warfare not by increasing bloodshed, but by concentrating it. Conflicts became less wandering, more deliberate.

Decisions once guided by seasons and survival shifted toward permanence. A leader who controlled gold could afford standing forces instead of temporary levies. Soldiers no longer fought only when crops allowed; they fought when commanded. Gold enabled continuity of force, and continuity of force enabled empire. Expansion became sustained rather than episodic. History lengthened its stride.

And yet, note this carefully. Gold did not make ancestors crueler. It made them *decisive*. When value endures, hesitation becomes expensive. Gold trained leaders to think in generations. To lose gold was to lose future options; to protect it was to protect tomorrow itself. Thus ancestral decisions hardened. Mercy thinned. Prudence thickened into suspicion.

Gold did not corrupt judgment; it *weighted* it.

In time, rituals formed around protection. Oaths sworn over gold. Treasuries blessed. Guards elevated to sacred duty. To protect gold was not merely a task, but a calling. Betrayal became sacrilege. Theft became treason. The metal restructured morality itself, teaching societies which crimes were unforgivable.

By the time empires learned to count years instead of seasons, gold had already trained them how to endure. It shaped not only where armies went, but how long they stayed, how deeply they dug in, how fiercely they defended what they claimed.

Thus gold's role in military and territorial history is not found in battles alone, but in the slow tightening of civilization's grip on itself. It taught men to guard, to refine, to fortify, and finally to believe that what is protected longest must be most valuable.

Whether this belief was wisdom or delusion remains unanswered.

But every wall ever raised, every standard ever carried, every territory ever held too long bears its fingerprint.

Gold did not make war inevitable. It made permanence desirable.

And once men learned to desire permanence, they were willing to fight for it without end.

CHAPTER IX: OF FIRE THAT LIED, SECRETS THAT BURNED, AND THE LEAD BURIED BENEATH GOLD

Alchemy was never merely the attempt to make gold. That is the lie told by those who arrived late and understood little. Alchemy was the first rebellion against the obvious. It was born when men realized that matter obeyed laws deeper than appearance, and that the world, like the soul, might be persuaded to become something other than what it seemed.

To the uninitiated, alchemy looked like madness: furnaces muttering in cellars, symbols scratched like heresies, men who trusted mercury more than priests. But beneath the smoke and superstition lay a dangerous intuition that transformation was not only possible, but *governed*. That lead was not damned eternally to baseness, nor gold eternally to purity, but that both were stages in a longer, hidden conversation between matter and time.

Thus gold became metaphor before it was product.

The alchemist did not seek wealth; he sought legitimacy in the eyes of the cosmos. To transmute was to prove that nature could be reasoned with, not merely endured. Fire became argument.

Vessels became grammar. Symbols stood in for truths too volatile to speak aloud. This is why alchemy clothed itself in magic—not to deceive, but to protect. Knowledge this subversive required camouflage.

To claim that matter could be perfected was to imply that authority could be questioned.

The legends multiplied accordingly. The philosopher's stone. The elixir of life. The green lion devouring the sun. These were not fantasies; they were encryptions. A language designed to survive persecution by remaining unintelligible to the literal-minded. Only those willing to suffer confusion were allowed clarity. Only those who accepted obscurity earned insight.

Yet obscurity did not guarantee safety.

Kings desired alchemists for the same reason they feared them. The promise of infinite gold was irresistible; the implication of infinite autonomy was intolerable. An alchemist who succeeded would be beyond taxation, beyond control. And so many were watched, confined, silenced—not because they failed, but because they *might not*.

Consider John of York, called of Goldthwaite, a quiet Englishman practicing his forbidden art in the fourteen hundreds. He was imprisoned for alchemy, accused not of fraud but of trespass against natural order. And yet here history betrays itself. He was soon released from the Tower of London. Why? Because the crown faced a shortage not of gold, but of *skill*. Coinage had to be minted. Metal had to be understood. Fire had to be obeyed.

The jailer needed the prisoner.

Thus alchemy survived not by triumph, but by indispensability. Its practitioners were alternately hunted and hired, condemned and consulted. Their knowledge was dangerous only when uncontrolled; when useful, it became invisible. The alchemist learned an early lesson that has never lost relevance: truth is persecuted until it is profitable, and then it is quietly absorbed.

Secrecy became survival.

This secrecy shaped not only alchemy, but gold's entire intellectual legacy. Knowledge about gold how it moves, how it concentrates, how it stabilizes power—was never destroyed. It was *buried.* Lead was placed atop it, metaphorically and literally, to discourage excavation by the unworthy. Complexity became camouflage. Institutions learned to speak loudly about surfaces while whispering about substance.

This is what modernity calls "burying the lead."

The essential truth of gold and its role as stabilizer of authority, as reservoir of optionality, as silent arbiter of trust was never denied. It was merely wrapped in layers of distraction: price charts, folklore, speculation, spectacle. Just as alchemists once hid equations inside dragons and suns, later ages hid gold's impact inside abstractions and noise.

Alchemy failed, they say. Yet metallurgy succeeded. Chemistry succeeded. Physics succeeded. And gold remained, unchanged, watching each discipline rediscover fragments of what the alchemist intuited whole.

What truly failed was honesty.

The alchemists were persecuted not because they lied, but because they spoke too close to the bone. They understood that transformation of metals, of men, of empires obeys rules that undermine complacency. And so their legacy persists not in laboratories, but in the structure of secrecy itself.

Gold still wears masks.

Knowledge still hides behind symbols.

Power still imprisons what it cannot afford to lose.

The furnaces are quieter now, the symbols more technical, the prisons more polite. But the pattern remains identical.

Alchemy did not disappear.

It professionalized and learned, at last, how to keep its mouth shut.

CHAPTER X: OF HIDDEN BULLION AND SILENT FORTRESSES

We stand at the edge of a golden abyss. The great nations of the earth, once proud in daylight, now hide behind the sealed vaults of their treasuries, trusting that no inquisition will dare to pry open their iron coffers. Thus the story of government gold audits is not merely the story of bars and bullion, but the story of secrecy, power, and the silent shaping of global destiny.

The Once-heralded Audits: Memory Fades

Long ago, the guardians of treasure dared to speak of transparency. In the United States, beginning in the mid-1970s the U.S. Department of the Treasury, following public pressure, authorized the Committee for Continuing Audit of the U.S. Government-owned Gold to conduct annual audits of government-owned gold. From roughly 1975 to 1986 this committee inspected and placed under official joint seal 97% of the gold then held by the Mint. But that vigilance dwindled. By 1993, formal auditing had faltered, and subsequent decades saw only cursory inspections; seals checked, vaults left unopened, gold itself unverified. Critics note that though official statements claim "audits," in practice such audits have become symbolic at best.

A later attempt at legislative oversight came in 2011, when Ron Paul introduced a measure to audit the gold reserves and publish results for public scrutiny. The bill died in the face of familiar opposition and the fortress of interests that prefer opacity over inquiry.

Since then it has been decades. No full, independent, public audit has verified that the gold remains pristine, unencumbered, and sovereign.

The Bearers of Gold: Who Holds the Most?

Meanwhile, the nations of the world cling tightly to their reported holdings. As of 2025, the top ten national holders of official gold reserves are, in descending order: United States (~ 8,133 tonnes), Germany (~ 3,351 t), Italy (~ 2,452 t), France (~ 2,437 t), Russia (~ 2,333 t), China (~ 2,280 t), Switzerland (~ 1,040 t), India, Japan, and Netherlands rounding out the top ten.

These numbers stand as the "official truth," The ledger-book version of reality. Yet they exist behind vault doors, behind seals, behind silence.

The Silence of Vaults: What an Absence of Audit Permits

Why has the practice of thorough audit vanished? Because to audit is to risk revelation. Liquidity & Leverage: If a nation's vault were proven empty or partly encumbered, the implied creditworthiness of that state would crumble. Keeping the reserves unexamined preserves an illusion of backing. A potent tool in global finance.

Financial Multiplicity: Gold held in vaults can be leased, swapped, refined, encumbered, all without public disclosure, while the books still claim "holds 8,133 tonnes." No audit: no reckoning.

Psychological Dominance: The myth of "massive gold reserves" buttresses confidence in fiat currencies or national currencies. It gives governments a silent war-chest of credibility, especially in times of crisis.

In short, secrecy preserves power. And power fears sunlight.

The Global Stage: Gold Reserves as a Hidden Axis of Influence

When the great holders of gold remain opaque, they steer not only their national economies, they shape the global gold market itself. Because gold is both commodity and myth, both asset and symbol.

Nations with unchallenged vaults signal strength, which affects investor sentiment, central-bank behavior, foreign exchange strategy. The unverified quantity acts as a form of leverage: in a crisis, the threat of "recalling" or "revaluing" hidden bullion can shift markets, currencies, even alliances. The uncertainty becomes speculative fuel: rumor, fear, confidence. All dancing around a secret mass of molten value buried under steel and secrecy. Thus gold becomes not just a reserve but a weapon of psychological and monetary influence.

The Path Forward Or the Abyss of Lies

I write this chapter as both testament and warning. Let those who hold the keys to the vaults consider this: the absence of audit is not empty neutrality, it is a void. A void filled with assumption, with faith, with ever-growing suspicion. If the guardians of gold would dare to show their treasures. To weigh, to assay, to open each vault, they might earn not only credibility but power based on truth. But if not, then let the world beware. Because what appears as solidity may be as hollow as a shell; and the value that men place on gold may prove to be the value of belief alone.

The Weight of Bullion: Data and Economic Resonance

Consider the vaults of nations. The hidden tonnage of bullion that no public eye may weigh. As of recent data, some of the world's great treasure-keepers hold astonishing quantities as listed earlier.

These hoards are not inert. They ripple through economies in manifold ways. Central banks and governments use gold reserves to stabilize currencies, to reassure markets, and to hedge against inflation and currency-debasement, thereby preserving purchasing power parity (PPP) inside their jurisdictions.

When fiat-money confidence wavers, gold remains a shelter. A store-of-value independent of political whim or debt mountains. Moreover, in times of crisis such as war, sanctions, capital flight, and external debt pressure, gold becomes a weapon of liquidity and sovereignty. Nations facing economic turbulence can lean on bullion to guarantee foreign-exchange commitments, restructure external debt, or act as collateral for international loans.

Historical precedents confirm the mortal value of such hidden gold. When a state's currency collapses or war ravages traditional financing channels then the cold, silent metal becomes the last refuge, the final trust. Thus: gold reserves influence not just balance sheets, but life and death of national economies, war-machinery, debt-structures, and public confidence.

GDP, Growth, Technological Advancements, and the Indirect Gravity of Gold

Though bullion itself does not mint GDP, its existence enables the very conditions under which growth, stability, and innovation may flourish or wither under crisis.

Macroeconomic Stability: Gold as a reserve reduces vulnerability to external shocks, inflation, and currency devaluation, thereby preserving a stable environment for investment, savings, and long-term planning. A stable macroeconomic climate is a precondition for industrial expansion, technological R&D, infrastructure, and human capital growth.

Fiscal and Sovereign Leverage: Nations with large reserves can secure more favorable credit, borrow on better terms, or avoid harsh defaults. This leverage supports large-scale public investments in defense, infrastructure, and science, all of which underpin technological advancement.

Crisis Buffer / War & Geopolitics: In periods when global capital flows seize or sanctions bite, gold offers a fallback. A nation whose vaults are full may still mobilize resources for war, defense, or reconstruction without depending on foreign financing or volatile markets. That war-financing capacity, ironically, becomes a pillar of long-term geopolitical and economic positioning. Historically, empires and states have financed wars and post-war recoveries by leaning on bullion or gold-backed reserves.

Psychological and Credibility Capital: When a nation is believed to have deep gold reserves, that belief fuels investor confidence, stabilizes currency value, and supports purchasing power.

That confidence encourages private investment, entrepreneurship, and innovation, which collectively drive GDP and technological productivity. Thus gold does not directly produce goods, but by anchoring the financial system, it shapes the fertile soil in which human creativity, enterprise, and progress can grow.

The Dark Benefit of Secrecy: Why Vaults Remain Closed

Yet the greatest economic value of gold for these nations lies in its secrecy. For if gold were audited, exposed, and weighed, then the world would not see a fortress but a ledger. And a ledger can be questioned, challenged, leveraged.

By keeping gold reserves unverified, opaque, unexamined, a state preserves:

1. Leverage through uncertainty. The possibility that vaults may be deeper than reported deters adversaries, instills market confidence, and sustains currency value without committing to spending that bullion. Flexibility for financial

maneuvers. Encumbering, leasing, swapping, collateralizing, all may be done off-book without public scrutiny, allowing states to use gold as a hidden line of credit when needed.

2. Psychological dominance. In debt negotiations, treaty bargaining, and war-time diplomacy, the mere myth of solid gold holdings provides weight. Markets and other nations treat gold-holders as safe, solvent, powerful.

In other words, secrecy transforms gold from a passive store-of-value into an active tool of monetary psychology, financial diplomacy, and sovereign strategy.

A System Tilted: Purchasing Power, PPP, Inequality, and Global Influence

When gold underpins or is perceived to underpin a nation's currency or reserves, that currency holds comparative stability. That stability reflects in purchasing power parity: citizens, investors, businesses enjoy a currency less prone to inflation, more predictable in global trade. Over decades, such stability fosters domestic savings, long-term investment, R&D, infrastructure, human development.

By contrast, nations without such reserves, or whose reserves are weak or exposed, face higher volatility: inflation, currency depreciation, unpredictable exchange-rates. These conditions imperil long-term planning, discourage large-scale investment, and make financing expensive. Moreover, on the global stage, bullion-rich, secret-vault nations dominate not only markets, but also directional narratives. Their gold reserves, whether verified or only rumored, become a silent axis around which currencies, trade-pacts, sanctions, geopolitical alignments rotate.

The Faustian Bargain: Gold, Fiat, and the Illusion of Stability

Yet this power comes at a cost. Gold no longer backs currency directly, (the classic "gold standard" having long been abandoned in most countries) still, nations treat bullion as symbolic collateral for fiat, debt, and modern financial constructs. Thus a paradox: gold is both real and myth, both anchor and illusion. Its weight anchors confidence, but its secrecy sustains the illusion.

The world trades in faith: faith that vaults are real, faith that reserves exist, faith that gold remains unencumbered. If the vaults were opened, if audits were real and public, the myth would die. Then what remains might be strength, or it might be emptiness. The entire global architecture, built on borrowed confidence and silent trust, might wobble.

In that balance lies the true power of gold: not the metal itself, but the knowledge and ignorance surrounding it.

CHAPTER XI: OF THE NEW ALCHEMISTS AND THE QUIET RETURN OF FIRE

The age of alchemy never ended. It only learned to pass inspections.

Today's alchemists do not wear robes or speak in suns and lions. They wear lab coats stained with patience, and they speak in parts per billion. They work not in towers but in sheds near small mines, in modular plants stitched together by necessity rather than capital. They do not promise miracles. They promise *yield*. And that humility makes them dangerous.

For these modern alchemists understand something the world pretends is simple and is not: that to separate gold, silver, and the platinum group metals without poisoning the land is not a matter of brute force, but of intimacy. They work at the nano scale, where surfaces matter more than mass, where chemistry persuades instead of assaults. No cyanide floods. No acid oceans. Instead, selectivity, ligands, temperature gradients, electrochemical whispers that coax atoms apart without wounding the host rock beyond forgiveness.

This knowledge is rare. Painfully rare.

The deficit is not in ore, nor in demand, nor even in capital. It is in *understanding*. Processing is the choke point of the modern metals world, just as transmutation was the choke point of medieval power. Mines may open easily enough, but refining. True refining remains an art guarded by few. Scaling such processes without surrendering ethics, efficiency, or control is the unsolved riddle that keeps boardrooms restless and landscapes scarred.

And where understanding is scarce, power concentrates.

Thus red tape begins to dissolve. Not out of enlightenment, but impatience. Environmental strictures soften their edges when compliance becomes too costly, too slow, too inconvenient. Regulations are rewritten in the language of "streamlining," which is merely another word for hunger with a tie on. The system, once rigid, now bends, and not toward wisdom, but toward throughput.

Yet even as permissions loosen, a subtler pressure tightens.

From startup to production, mining operations feel the same quiet push: *sell early, sell abroad, sell control.* Refining capacity lags domestically; buyers wait elsewhere with open hands and quicker furnaces. Metals leave their birthplace not because it is logical, but because it is *necessary*. The ore departs before it learns its final form. Value is exported not by decree, but by absence of capability.

Here the ancient pattern returns intact.

Those who hold proprietary knowledge within true separation, clean refinement, independent sale, hold sovereignty without banners. They need no armies. Their leverage is optionality. They can wait. They can choose. They can refuse. This is the same leverage once whispered about philosopher's stones and infinite gold not through abundance, but autonomy.

And like the alchemists before them, these practitioners live in contradiction. Celebrated quietly when needed. Ignored when inconvenient. Suspected always. Their methods are scrutinized, patented, regulated, appropriated. Their successes are praised until they threaten incumbents, and then the language shifts. What was innovation becomes "risk." What was stewardship becomes "unscalable." What was progress becomes "nonstandard."

Persecution no longer wears chains. It wears audits.

The mystery remains because the problem remains the same: whoever controls transformation controls dependency. Early alchemists frightened kings because they suggested money need not obey lineage. Modern alchemists unsettle systems because they suggest extraction need not obey destruction, and value need not obey foreign hands. In both cases, the threat is not fraud, but *independence.*

Science advances, yet secrecy persists. The symbols are cleaner now. Formulas emerged instead of glyphs, but the instinct to conceal remains unchanged. Knowledge that collapses margins is buried under jargon. Processes that liberate landscapes are stalled under compliance. And the essential truth that extraction can be precise, humane, and sovereign is diluted before it can coagulate into power.

Thus the struggle repeats, refined but familiar.

Alchemy was once dismissed as superstition because it asked the wrong question too early: *Can matter be perfected?* Today's alchemists ask the right question too quietly: *Can value be retained without surrender?* And for this, they inherit the same loneliness, the same suspicion, the same necessity for silence.

Fire still teaches, but only those who listen learn.

The land waits. The metals wait. The knowledge exists, but like gold itself, it concentrates where pressure is greatest and visibility is lowest.

And as always, the future belongs not to those who dig the most, but to those who know what to do with what they uncover and who can keep that knowledge long enough to choose their moment.

CHAPTER XII: OF THE HAND THAT HOLDS AND THE WEIGHT THAT LIBERATES

The masses do not need to know how gold is made. They never have. Knowledge of furnaces and formulas has always belonged to the few, and it is no insult to say this. It is simply the architecture of civilization. One does not need to understand the anatomy of the sun to feel its warmth. One does not need to know the mathematics of gravity to stand upright. And one does not need to trace neutron capture through dying stars to understand what gold *does* when it is held.

Gold works without explanation.

What matters to the many is not process, but participation. Not metallurgy, but meaning. When individuals choose gold, quietly, personally, without banners or permission, they alter the field in which value itself moves. Each act of holding is small, almost laughably so, and yet the aggregate becomes irresistible. This is not magic; it is economics stripped of illusion. Demand that is voluntary, distributed, and patient reshapes price not through coercion, but through conviction.

Gold does not rise because men agree it should. It rises because men *act* as though it matters.

When individuals buy gold, they do not merely hedge themselves; they stabilize one another. Value ceases to be a decree and becomes a consensus of touch. The more hands that choose weight over promise, the more weight remembers itself. This is how gold increases in value for everyone by removing itself from circulation, by refusing velocity, by slowing the frantic churn of abstraction. Gold appreciates not by moving faster, but by *stopping*.

In this stillness, secrets unlock.

For gold is one of the few objects whose meaning deepens when possessed rather than displayed. It does not ask to be shown. It does not need witnesses. Its metaphysical gravity reveals itself privately, in the palm, in the subtle recalibration of one's relationship to time. To hold gold is to feel duration made dense. It presses gently downward, reminding the nervous system of permanence in a world addicted to motion.

This sensation is not taught. It is *felt*.

And what is felt reshapes belief more reliably than any doctrine. Gold has leveraged nations and territories not because it glittered, but because it endured when everything else negotiated.

Empires bent around it, currencies leaned against it, wars paused for it. To hold gold is to touch the same invariant that once anchored borders and restrained ambition. The individual feels without needing to articulate that they are holding something older than law and quieter than force.

This is where democratization enters—not as politics, but as physics.

Gold democratizes value because it does not care who holds it. It recognizes no credentials, no ideology, no allegiance. The smallest piece carries the same truth as the largest bar. When individuals choose gold, the future of the dollar, and of money itself ceases to belong exclusively to institutions and returns, fraction by fraction, to hands. Not equal outcomes, but equal *access* to the same invariant measure.

This is democracy in its original sense: power diffused, not centralized; choice exercised, not granted.

Free will requires options that are not revocable. Gold provides this without speech. It does not promise freedom; it *permits* it. The freedom to wait. The freedom to move. The freedom to refuse unfavorable terms. These freedoms do not announce themselves. They are discovered only after possession, when the holder realizes that something in their posture toward the world has shifted.

One stands differently when one owns something that does not need permission to be valuable.

This is why the masses need not understand extraction, refining, or scale. Those are concerns of fire and secrecy. What the many need is contact. Participation. The quiet alignment that occurs when millions independently choose the same anchor, not because they were instructed, but because they sensed gravity.

Gold has always been a teacher that does not speak.

It teaches patience to the restless, humility to the ambitious, and sovereignty to the cautious. It reminds the holder, without ceremony, that freedom is not granted by systems, but accumulated through choices that resist erosion.

And when you hold it, really hold it, you feel something that no explanation can improve upon: the calm recognition that you are touching a fragment of catastrophe turned into order, of chaos reconciled into weight, of history condensed into silence.

The secrets were never hidden.

They were simply too heavy to be carried by those unwilling to pick them up.

CHAPTER XIII: THE YEAR THE GODS WENT SILENT

There are years in history when nations change course not with the thunder of armies, but with the quiet click of a pen. 1971 was such a year. A year when an old god, gold itself, was dismissed from the temple and told it would no longer speak for the dollar. And like all dethroned gods, its silence echoed.

For decades prior, the world had been bound by a strange priesthood of accountants and statesmen. Their altar was not Olympus but a hotel in New Hampshire, and their theology was simple: Peg the world to America, and America to gold, and thus build peace through dependence. It was a noble lie, perhaps even a clever one. But the lie held, and the world prospered until it didn't.

Because beneath this golden altar, something was rotting.

Wages lagged while productivity marched forward like an unthinking soldier. Homes transmuted from shelter into speculative idols.

Savings thinned.

Debt fattened.

And inequality eternal, patient inequality rose like a forgotten titan.

Some claim that this decay began precisely when Nixon severed gold from the dollar. But this is only partly true. It is the weakness of the herd to believe in a single villain, a single moment, a single fall from grace. It flatters the mind into thinking the world was simple once. But the world was never simple. Only our illusions were.

Gold convertibility had already become a farce, a mask stretched over contradictions: too many dollars, too little gold, too many nations calling America's bluff. The French, arrogant as always, simply said the quiet part aloud: "Let us see the gold. Let us test this privilege." And when they sent their battleship to New York Harbor to collect it, the masquerade was over.

One cannot demand reverence once others have glimpsed the empty sanctuary. So Nixon ended the pretense. He removed the "training wheels," as some now mockingly say. Without them, the economy flew faster, climbed higher, and inevitably crashed harder. Wealth accumulated at the top like snow on a mountaintop while the valleys below darkened and chilled. The charts spiked, dipped, and twisted, and the people, ever trusting in patterns, searched desperately for someone to blame.

But the truth is more complex, more uncomfortable:

After 1971 came the true revolution. Not of metals but of markets, not of currencies but of power.

The 1980s arrived with the force of a new philosophy:

Break the unions.

Unleash the monopolies.

Worship the shareholder.

Privatize the public.

And call this freedom.

Gold did not do this.

Gold merely stepped aside, and into the vacuum strode bolder gods; profit, scale, efficiency, growth. Titans born of silicon, satellites, shipping containers, and deregulation. And the people, dazzled by abundance, did not notice that the ground beneath them had changed shape.

Yet look closely at the graphs of our age. They bent sharply in the 1970s not because evil entered the world, but because compounding finally revealed its teeth. What looks like catastrophe is sometimes only mathematics awakening from its slumber. Still, the myth persists: "If only we had kept the gold, all would be well." But this longing is merely another form of cowardice.

Nostalgia dressed in economic theory.Man wants a fixed point in a spinning world, a weight to hold against the tides of inflation, inequality, and uncertainty. Gold is honest. Gold is finite.

Gold resists the whims of men.

And so men dream of returning to it, as though returning to a stern father after years of indulgence.

But history offers no return, only transformation. The gold standard did not collapse because humanity grew wicked. It collapsed because humanity grew large. Too large to be contained by a

system designed for a smaller world. Growth is always purchased with disorder. Freedom is always purchased with risk. And so the great question of our time is not:

"Should we go back?"

but rather:

"What new gods will we create to replace the old?"

For gold will endure. It always has. But its rule, its

empire over money, has passed. And in its absence, men have learned a terrible, exhilarating truth:

When no metal restrains us, we become responsible for restraining ourselves. A responsibility we have not yet mastered.

Gold is not discovered by desire.

It is revealed by pressure. Geological, political, and moral.

Those who understand *where* gold sleeps shape the future long before a single ounce is mined. And those who mistake possession for wisdom inevitably awaken it too early.

www.ingramcontent.com/pod-product-compliance
Lightning Source LLC
LaVergne TN
LVHW022028200926
848481LV00007B/2594